by Mignonne Gunasekara
& Charis Mather

Minneapolis, Minnesota

Credits
Images are courtesy of Shutterstock.com. With thanks to Getty Images, Thinkstock Photo, and iStockphoto.
RECURRING – Amovitania. COVER – NotionPic. 4–5 – Noah Sydnor, Elena Blanes. 6–7 – Vadim Petrakov, Richard Constantinoff. 8–9 – Andy Wasley, CreativeNature_nl, Martin Hibberd. 10–11 – fernando sanchez, Robert Adamec. 12–13 – Barbara Ash, Charidy Bunsa. 14–15 – Erni, Dilomski. 16–17 – CDK Photos, Martine Liu 58. 18–19 – Peter Wey, BCBimages. 20–21 – Chris Hill, Harry Collins Photography. 22–23 – scott mirror, Birdiegal, Mike van Kal. 24 – BCBimages.

Bearport Publishing Company Product Development Team
President: Jen Jenson; Director of Product Development: Spencer Brinker; Managing Editor: Allison Juda; Associate Editor: Naomi Reich; Associate Editor: Tiana Tran; Art Director: Colin O'Dea; Designer: Elena Klinkner; Designer: Kayla Eggert; Product Development Assistant: Owen Hamlin

Library of Congress Cataloging-in-Publication Data

Names: Gunasekara, Mignonne, author. | Mather, Charis, 1999- author.
Title: Brutal birds / by Mignonne Gunasekara & Charis Mather.
Description: Roar! books. | Minneapolis, Minnesota : Bearport Publishing Company, [2024] | Series: Powerful predators | Includes index.
Identifiers: LCCN 2023035146 (print) | LCCN 2023035147 (ebook) | ISBN 9798889165736 (library binding) | ISBN 9798889165781 (paperback) | ISBN 9798889165828 (ebook)
Subjects: LCSH: Birds of prey--Juvenile literature.
Classification: LCC QL677.78 .G86 2024 (print) | LCC QL677.78 (ebook) | DDC 598.9--dc23/eng/20230824
LC record available at https://lccn.loc.gov/2023035146
LC ebook record available at https://lccn.loc.gov/2023035147

© 2024 BookLife Publishing
This edition is published by arrangement with BookLife Publishing.

North American adaptations © 2024 Bearport Publishing Company. All rights reserved. No part of this publication may be reproduced in whole or in part, stored in any retrieval system, or transmitted in any form or by any means, electronic, mechanical, photocopying, recording, or otherwise, without written permission from the publisher.

For more information, write to Bearport Publishing, 5357 Penn Avenue South, Minneapolis, MN 55419.

CONTENTS

WELCOME TO THE WORLD OF PREDATORS

Predators are everywhere in the animal world.

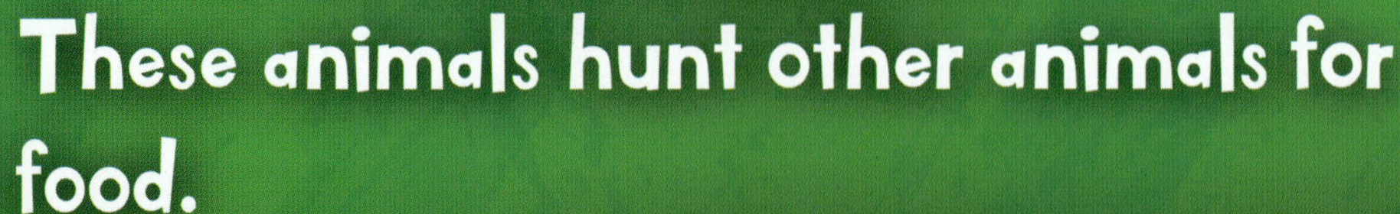

These animals hunt other animals for food.

Some birds are powerful predators. Their **prey** does not stand a chance!

Get ready to meet **brutal** birds.

POWERFUL GREAT WHITE PELICANS

Great white pelicans are large birds with stretchy pouches under their bills.

They scoop up fish in these pouches.

Great white pelicans hunt by swimming in circles around their prey.

This way, the fish cannot escape. Then, it is time to eat.

CRUEL COMMON KESTRELS

Kestrels are not very big, but they are still dangerous hunters.

Common kestrels can **hover** in the air. They hunt from high above.

These predators eat small animals, including other birds.

BEASTLY BARN OWLS

Barn owls are most active at night. Their good hearing helps them find prey, even in the dark.

Barn owls can fly very quietly to sneak up on prey.

They **attack** with their hooked beaks and sharp **talons**.

SAVAGE SECRETARY BIRDS

Unlike most birds, secretary birds do not hunt from the air.

They chase after their prey on the ground.

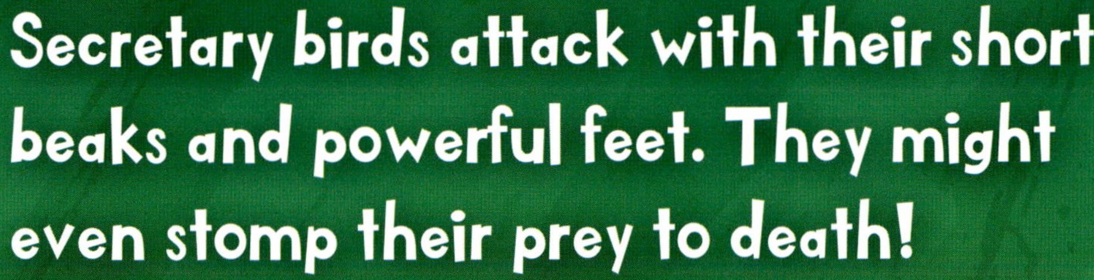

Secretary birds attack with their short beaks and powerful feet. They might even stomp their prey to death!

SCARY GREAT SKUAS

The great skua is a brutal bird that lives by the coast.

This large seabird has a sharp beak and talons.

Great skuas hunt fish swimming near the surface of the water.

They also **steal** food from other birds.

KILLER COMMON
KINGFISHERS

Do not let the small size of the common kingfisher fool you.

These brutal birds hunt fish and insects near slow-moving water.

Common kingfishers spot fish while sitting on **perches** near the water. Then, they quickly dive down to catch their prey.

EAGER BALD EAGLES

Bald eagles have very good eyesight. They can see prey from far away.

Once they spot fish in the water, these birds use their long, sharp talons to grab their prey.

They rip into the meal with their hooked beaks.

Frightening Peregrine Falcons

Peregrine falcons hunt other birds, such as pigeons.

Their sharp talons make them scary predators. So does their speed!

A hunting peregrine falcon may dive toward its prey. The bird can go 200 miles per hour (320 kph).

BRUTAL AND BEASTLY

Birds hunt in many different ways.

Some snatch prey from the skies.

Others scoop food from the sea.

There are even birds that grab their prey on the ground.

They are all brutal in their own way!

Glossary

attack to cause harm

brutal extremely tough or difficult

hover to stay in one place in the air

perches places above the ground where people or animals can sit or stand

prey animals that are hunted for food

steal to take by force

talons sharp claws

Index